# Abandonings

## Photographs of Otter Tail County, Minnesota

*by* MAXWELL MACKENZIE

*Elliott & Clark Publishing, Washington DC*

*For their support of this project I am indebted to*

Theodore Adamstein & Olvia Demetriou
Eason & Diana Cross
Stephen Davis DeTuerk
John Dreyfuss & Mary Noble Ours
Mark Edmundson & Elizabeth Denton
Linnea Hamer
David & Mary W. Lundeen
Edward Lundeen
Elizabeth Ernst Meyer & Michael McCaffrey
Bill & Alison Paley
Michael Pollan
Julie Saul
Ruth Lundeen MacKenzie Saxe
Frank Van Riper

The American Architectural Foundation
*Architecture Minnesota*
Fuji Photo Film USA, Inc.
Maryland Federation of Art
National Building Museum
Otter Tail County Historical Society
The Virginia Foundation for Architecture
The Washington Project for the Arts

Abandonings
*Photographs of Otter Tail County, Minnesota*
MAXWELL MACKENZIE

Published by Elliott & Clark Publishing,
PO Box 21038, Washington, DC 20009-0538

Photographs copyright © 1995 by Maxwell MacKenzie,
2641 Garfield Street NW, Washington, DC 20008

ISBN 1-880216-34-5
Printed in Hong Kong through Mandarin Offset
Designed by Bogart Szabo Design Inc., Washington DC
Third printing

*I am, like all sons who become fathers,*

*one link in a chain that stretches infinitely out in two directions,*

*disappearing backward into the forgotten*

*and forward into the unknown,*

*with the one becoming the other at a frightening pace.*

*To those of my ancestors and descendants who have known and loved Otter Tail,*

*especially the farthest links in each direction*

*whose lives have overlapped my own:*

*to the memory of my grandfather, Victor George Lundeen (1898-1985),*

*to my two young sons, Alexander and Cooper,*

*and to my loving wife Rebecca,*

*without whose energy, enthusiasm, and help*

*these photographs would never have been made,*


*I dedicate this book.*

IN THE YEAR that I turned forty, I returned to the place where I was born, though not raised, and was drawn to make photographs of the remnants of an earlier life there, now all but passed away. ❧ Otter Tail County lies northwest of Minneapolis-St. Paul, close to the North Dakota border, on the edge of the Great Plains. Europeans first settled there in 1865, and over the next fifty years, thousands came, primarily Norwegians and Swedes. Among them was my great-grandfather, Lars Erick Lundeen, who came in 1880 at the age of twenty-one. Most of the immigrants were farmers who took advantage of the free land, rich black earth, and abundant water. ❧ By the 1930s, many of the pioneers had already begun to leave the land, forced by dust storms and the Depression to desert the very homes they had struggled so hard to build. As I drove the hundreds of back roads,

I felt the need to document some of what remains before all traces disappear and we have no reminders of what went before. I wanted us to remember their brave efforts and the graceful shelters they built, even in ruin so pleasing to the eye. ❧ To me, this landscape and these buildings —sad, empty, silent houses and falling-down barns – possess a profound beauty, not merely for their spare, simple designs and weathered boards, but as monuments to the men and women who, like my own ancestors, made long journeys and endured great hardships to reach this remote part of America and build in it a new home.

MAXWELL MACKENZIE

The country derived its name from Otter Tail Lake and River which in turn were given their names by the Chippewa Indians who saw a likeness to an otter's tail in the shape of the prominent bar that extends into the Lake.

MINNESOTA HISTORICAL RECORDS 1940 ❧ *Survey Project*

*plate* I

My grandparents had to live their way out of
one world and into another, or into several others,
making new out of old the way corals live their
reef upward.  I am on my grandparents' side.
I believe in Time, as they did, and in the life
chronological rather than in the life existential.
We live in time and through it, we build our
huts in its ruins, or used to, and we cannot
afford all these abandonings.


WALLACE STEGNER          ❧  1971

*Angle of Repose*

*plate* 2

. . . the first snow falls on the prairie;  snow filters between the brown rotted stalks of frozen stubble, then snow calks the unending seams of summer-fallowed earth, then snow slips through the barbed-wire, fills the wide, deep, straight ditches, spills across the falling fans of lath fences; snow wraps softly the wheel of the world and stops the wheel of the merry-go-round.  It will not stop falling, even though all the children inside the schoolhouse are willing it to stop until the recess bell rings, for fear there will not be any left to fall on them when their minutes of liberty come.

LOIS PHILLIPS HUDSON    &  1965

*Reapers of the Dust: A Prairie Chronicle*

The reactions that many experience toward
the plain, regular geometry of balloon frame
farmhouses resonates with an admiration
for what is perceived and valued as a simple,
certain way of life.  This simplicity, however . . .
was the outcome of a harsh and unrelenting
effort to realize desired results by employing the
least means.  Certainty arose from convictions
based on truths tested in the difficulties of one's
own experience and the successes and failures
of others.  Here was an ingrained standard for
beauty and a practical test for truth.

1992  &  FRED W. PETERSON

*Homes in the Heartland*

*plate 3*

*plate* 4

East of the creek, framed houses were rising above the sod huts . . . . The new houses seemed so out of place, standing up on the open, bare prairie. Did they really belong there? They looked so defiant! . . . And that was exactly what the savage storm thought when he came along, winter or summer, found these unheard-of-objects in his way, puffed and wheezed, took firm hold, and roared in anger. Well, perhaps he did more than that; it happened now and then that a house would be toppled over, or shattered and torn to pieces; but no matter how hard the storm raged and fumed and growled and took on about it, most of the houses remained standing, and their numbers steadily increased as the years went by.

O. E. Rolvaag        1924

*Giants in the Earth*

There may be as good ways to understand the
shape and intensity of the dream that peopled the
continent, but this seems to me one good one.
How does one know in his bones what this
continent has meant to Western man unless he
has, though briefly and in the midst of failure,
belatedly and in the wrong place, made trails and
paths on an untouched country and built human
living places, however transitory, at the edge of
a field that he helped break from prairie sod?

1955 &a.        WALLACE STEGNER
                *Wolf Willow*

*plate* 6

*plate* 7

My father and grandfather would often speak of
the earlier days . . . of tornadoes that switched
the roofs of barns and houses, and of hailstorms
that rained sheep-killing stones, heaping July
wheatfields with desolations of ice.

Even more fascinating to me were their stories
of the early winters.  I would never see any
winters like these, they said, for a new and milder
weather cycle now prevailed.  I would never know
the bitter years that built the grim legends of our
northern land.

My mother used to tell me how once a prairie
wolf had stalked her as she walked home alone
from school, over miles of abandoned stubble.

LOIS PHILLIPS HUDSON        1965

*Reapers of the Dust: A Prairie Chronicle*

*plate* 9

Some had given up after the first blizzard.
Others had trailed away through the mud and ice
of March. Now each time we went to Gary we
heard about still others who had waited only for
spring to get up and go. There was the man
who got on his horse one afternoon and told his
wife he was going to bring in the cows. She
watched him ride off across the flats. He came
to their two mild cows, grazing half-a-mile from
the house, and he rode around them and kept on
going. She watched him to the top of the rise,
a mile away, and she waited and waited. He never
came back. "I don't know what got into him,"
his wife said. "He didn't even say goodbye."

HAL BORLAND 🐌 1956

*High, Wide and Lonesome*

There were grasshopper years when . . . we got nothing. The first time they came the crops were looking wonderful. Wheat fields so green and corn way up. The new ploughed fields yielded marvelously and . . . the talk was all in praise of this new country and the crops. While we were talking it gradually darkened. The men hastily went out to see if anything should be brought in before the storm. What a sight when we opened the door! The sky darkened by myriads of grasshoppers and no green thing to be seen . . . . Everything was gone. By the middle of the afternoon, when they left, the wheat fields looked as if they had been burned, even the roots eaten. Not a leaf on the trees . . . . Back of the house where they had flown against it they were piled up four feet high.

1856 ❧   MRS. JANE SUTHERLAND

*Old Rail Fence Corners: Frontier Tales
Told by Minnesota Pioneers*

*plate* 10

*plate* II

The winters were very long and severely cold and many times they would be shut in by the depth of the snow for weeks at a time. One time in particular the snow was so deep and the cold so intense that they had been snowbound for so long that their supplies were almost exhausted, and my grandfather sent the men off to get a fresh supply. They were gone much longer than usual and the little family began to suffer for want of food and were obliged to go out and scrape away the snow to find acorns. They also ate the bark off the trees.

MRS. W. L. NIEMANN          ❧ 1857

*Old Rail Fence Corners: Frontier Tales
Told by Minnesota Pioneers*

*plate* 12

There was the man, who as soon as the last snow was gone and the roads were open, took his wife to Brush to get a load of groceries, and 100 pounds of chicken feed. He gave her the grocery money and let her off at the store, saying he would get the chicken feed and meet her there in half an hour. Meanwhile the Denver train came in and left. When the man went back to the store to meet his wife, she wasn't there. He couldn't find a trace of her, until he went to the depot and described her to the station agent. Yes, the agent said, he'd seen a woman like that. She bought a ticket and she got on the train. And the man walked out, dazed, and got in his wagon and drove home again.

HAL BORLAND     1956

*High, Wide and Lonesome*

*plate* 13

My mother told of a storm in her childhood . . .
there were no roads, no telephones or radio – just
homesteader shacks scattered over the prairie.
The storm came up quickly on a nice afternoon
and kept getting worse until it turned into a
raging blizzard. They had the oxen in the sod
barn and weren't able to get to the barn for 8 days
to feed them . . . . Firewood was impossible to
get at so they burned much of their partitions in
the house and some furniture to keep warm.
They rationed their food and melted snow for
water . . . . The frost collected on the inside walls
of their house to a thickness of 4 inches . . . .
After 8 days my grandfather was able to get to the
barn by stretching a clothes line from the house to
avoid getting lost in the swirling snow. They
found the livestock alive but gaunt.

RUSSELL DUNCAN        ❧  1980

*The Day of the Pioneer*

. . . the groves of trees which the settlers had striven so hard to plant and rear – they stretched and spread, they grew in height and breadth and richness every summer.  As they grew, they hid the houses, except where the driveway was to come in, when plans and visions became reality.  There were settlers, even, who wooded themselves in so completely – perhaps to keep out all evil – that their houses could not be seen at all until one came inside the grove.

1924           O. E. ROLVAAG

*Giants in the Earth*

*plate* 15

But dearest to him of all, and most delectable,
was the thought of the royal mansion which he
had already erected in his mind. There would be
houses for both chickens and pigs, roomy
stables, a magnificent storehouse and barn . . .
and then the splendid palace itself! The royal
mansion would shine in the sun – it would stand
out far and wide! The palace itself would be
white, with green cornices; but the big barn
would be as red as blood, with cornices of
driven snow. Wouldn't it be beautiful – wasn't
it going to be great fun! . . . and he and
his boys would build it all.

1924    O. E. ROLVAAG
*Giants in the Earth*

*plate* 16

*plate* 18

There was plenty of good timber . . . but the settlers were farmers who had little or no experience in cutting and dressing logs and for that reason handled their few small tools to poor advantage. They were anxious, too, to be 'breaking' the prairie so that a crop could be harvested that first year. So, after all, these first houses were rather poor specimens of the joiner's craft. I was a carpenter and put up a rather more substantial house than the others, but none too comfortable during the winters that were to follow. The unbroken stretch of prairie to the north and west . . . gave those old 'northwesters' a splendid sweep before they struck our frail little homes.

MR. MICHAEL TEETER        1857

*Old Rail Fence Corners: Frontier Tales Told by Minnesota Pioneers*

In the congested districts it seems to be everyone for himself. On the frontier a settler becomes ill and his grain is sown, planted and harvested. Who by? Neighbors. A widow buries her husband and again the neighbors come. It is no light thing for one to leave his own harvest and go miles to save the crop of another, but it is and has been done times without number . . . and the sentiment which prompts such kindly acts counts for something . . . in making up the sum total of happiness in this short life of ours.

1859     JUDGE LORIN CRAY

*Old Rail Fence Corners: Frontier Tales*
*Told by Minnesota Pioneers*

*plate* 19

*plate* 20

There are poems, sometimes written by people
riding a train from one ocean to the other across
that stricken expanse of abandoned continent,
which celebrate the pathos of a house abandoned
in the blowing fields, but I have never seen a
poem which deals with the day on which a child
of that house is sent out for half a bucket of
water and comes running back through the dust
to report that the well is dry.

LOIS PHILLIPS HUDSON　　🐦　1965

*Reapers of the Dust: A Prairie Chronicle*

Finally my grandfather concluded that he, too, must start out to try and get some food. The windows of the cabin were covered in place of glass, with deerskins. In getting ready to leave the children, grandfather took down those skins and replaced them with blankets to keep out the cold and boiled the skins to provide a soup for the children to drink while he was gone. My mother was twelve and her sister was ten.

1857   MRS. W. L. NIEMANN

*Old Rail Fence Corners: Frontier Tales*
*Told by Minnesota Pioneers*

*plate* 21

All prairie people, like desert people, can recognize from a great distance the elongated dots of their kind.  They know, when a speck appears on the unchanging rim of the world, whether or not it is human . . . .

I had always believed that it was the ones who had gone before me who understood the circle and where they belonged in it, but instead they supposed that it was the ones coming after them who would understand.

We learn one thing from the ones who came before us:  how to recognize the dots of our own kind in all the space that is between us.  And that recognition is all there can be.  As for the secrets – we inherit them with the earth.  The hidden is never revealed.  Rather, it is the lost secrets of the old people that give the earth its dreadful beauty.

1965  &  LOIS PHILLIPS HUDSON

*Reapers of the Dust: A Prairie Chronicle*

*plate* 22

*plate* 24

My father . . . left his home in New York state
and came to Minnesota in 1854. The next year
he decided to go after his family and so wrote
my mother to be ready to start in August . . . .
I shall never forget the shock I felt at the first
view I had of our new home. It was so different
from what we had left behind, that to a child of
my age, it seemed that it was more than I could
possibly endure. It was growing dark and the
little log cabin stood in the deep woods and
the grass was so long in the front yard, it
seemed the most lonely place in the world . . . .
In the morning, when the house was in order
and the sun was shining in, and we could see
what father had done to make us comfortable,
the place took on a very different aspect and
soon became another dear home.

MRS. EDMUND KIMBALL          1855

*Old Rail Fence Corners: Frontier Tales*
*Told by Minnesota Pioneers*

. . . at our auction we were obliged to shrink on the outskirts of the small group of farmers . . . who made humiliating bids on the sad trappings of our permanence and bought them at sums that made my mother's eyes seek my father's in frightened dismay. We had counted on getting much more to help us move to another place where there would not be so many enemies of roots.

1965   LOIS PHILLIPS HUDSON

*Reapers of the Dust: A Prairie Chronicle*

*plate* 25

We built a log cabin with 'chinkins' to let in the air. We filled in the cracks except where these chinkins were, with mud. The roof was made by laying popple poles so they met in the middle and fastening them together. Over this were laid a heavy thickness of wild hay, and over that the popple poles again well tied with hand twisted ropes of wild hay, to those below. It was a good roof, only it leaked like a sieve. The floor was just the ground. Over it we put a layer of the wild hay and then staked a rag carpet over it. A puncheon shelf to put my trunk under, and the furniture placed, made a home that I was more than satisfied with . . . . My baby was born three weeks after we moved in. There was no doctor within a hundred miles. I got through, helped only by my sister-in-law. What do you women nowadays, with your hospitals and doctors, know of a time like this?

1854   MRS. MARTHA THORNE

*Old Rail Fence Corners: Frontier Tales*
*Told by Minnesota Pioneers*

*plate* 26

Acknowledgments

*Angle of Repose*
© 1971 Wallace Stegner
Reprinted by permission of Doubleday, a division of Bantam Doubleday Dell Publishing Group, Inc.

*Wolf Willow*
© 1955, 1957, 1958, 1959, 1962 Wallace Stegner
Copyright renewed 1990 by Wallace Stegner
Reprinted by permission of Brandt & Brandt Literary Agents, Inc.

*Reapers of the Dust: A Prairie Chronicle*
© 1965, 1984 by Lois Phillips Hudson
Reprinted by permission of the Minnesota Historical Society Press

*Giants in the Earth*
© 1924 O. E. Rolvaag
Reprinted by permission of Harper Perennial/Harper Collins

*Old Rail Fence Corners: Frontier Tales Told by Minnesota Pioneers*
Lucy L. W. Morris, Editor
Minnesota Society of the Daughters of the American Revolution, 1914
Reprint edition © 1976, Reprinted by permission of the Minnesota Historical Society Press

*High, Wide & Lonesome*
© 1965 Hal Borland
Reprinted by permission of Harper Perennial/Harper Collins

*Homes in the Heartland: Balloon Frame Farmhouses of the Upper Midwest, 1850-1920*
© 1992 Fred W. Peterson
Reprinted by permission of the University Press of Kansas

*The Day of the Pioneer*
© 1980 Russell Duncan, author and publisher

*The true basis for any serious study of the art of architecture still lies in those indigenous, more humble buildings everywhere that are to architecture what folklore is to literature and folk song to music.*

FRANK LLOYD WRIGHT

*Index to Photographic Plates*

*plate* 28

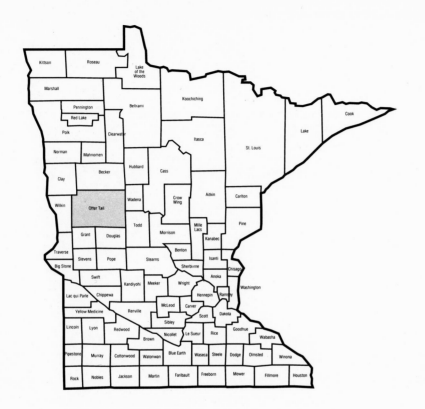

The fine scenery of lake and open groves of oak timber, of winding stream connecting them, and beautiful rolling country on all sides renders this portion of Minnesota the garden spot of the Northwest.

CAPTAIN JOHN POPE          🐾     1849

*U.S. Topographical Engineers' Survey of the Area which became Otter Tail County*